CALVINISM, ARMINIANISM & THE WORD OF GOD

A CALVARY CHAPEL PERSPECTIVE

CHUCK SMITH

THE WORD
FOR TODAY

P.O. Box 8000, Costa Mesa, CA 92628
Website: www.twft.com
E-mail: info@twft.com

Calvinism, Arminianism, and the Word of God
A Calvary Chapel Perspective

by Chuck Smith

© 1993, 2002, 2004 The Word For Today Publishers, P.O. Box 8000, Costa Mesa, CA 92628

Web Site: www.twft.com

ISBN 0-936728-46-9

Unless otherwise indicated, all scripture quotations are taken from the King James Version of the Bible. Translation emendations, amplifications, and paraphrases are by the author.

Printed in the United States of America.

Trust in the Lord

with all thine heart;

and lean not unto

thine own understanding.

PROVERBS 3:5

CALVINISM, ARMINIANISM
& THE WORD OF GOD

What does it mean to be a part of the growing number of Calvary Chapel Fellowships? There are certain distinctions that cause us to stand out among other evangelical churches. We could point to our shared commitment to systematic Bible teaching or the emphasis upon love that transcends all cultural and ethnic barriers. Calvary Chapels have also been known for focus on worship, featuring contemporary music loyal to the Word of God and the desire of His people to praise their Lord. Without exception, Calvary Chapels have taken a strong stand for a pre–tribulational and pre–millennial view of the second coming of Jesus Christ. We have also expressed a steadfast love and support for the nation of Israel, its right to a historic homeland and its need for the Messiah. But most importantly, Calvary Chapel has been known for striking a balance between extremes on controversial theological issues that have often caused division rather than unity in the body of Christ.

Calvary Chapels have no desire to be divisive nor dogmatic in areas where Bible believers and teachers have disagreed. However, it is important to state as clearly as possible the doctrinal basis of our fellowship and unity with one another, especially in the area of pastoral leadership and teaching. While we welcome believers who disagree with us to our fellowship, we do encourage a measure of doctrinal understanding and unity among our pastors who teach us the truths of God's Word.

Calvary Chapels try to avoid conclusions, terminology, and arguments which are not clearly presented in the Bible. In no area of controversy is this approach more essential than in the long simmering debate between Calvinists and Arminians. In the midst of this heated argument it is easy to ignore or neglect the plain statements of the Bible, or to believe that we have the ability to fully understand the ways of God (Romans 11:33–36). But how tragic it is when we become more concerned with being "right" than being loving. When we discuss the ministry of the Holy Spirit, it is easy to disagree over terms such as "baptism" and "filling" and to miss the blessing and power of God's Spirit in our lives. The way we conduct our debates and express our opinions will sometimes "quench" as well as "grieve" the blessed Spirit who dwells within the believer. In the midst of our arguments over spiritual gifts, we can miss the Biblical admonition to love, which clearly is greater than all the gifts (I Cor. 12:31–14:1). Our desire is to bring believers together in the love and unity of the Holy Spirit. Our focus is on our awesome God, not on ourselves. We are committed to glorifying our Lord in all we say and do.

Perhaps no issue is as important or as potentially divisive as the doctrine of salvation, reflected in the debate between followers of John Calvin (1509–1564) and those of Jacob Hermann (1560–1609), best known by the Latin form of his last name, Arminius. Since the Protestant Reformation in the 16th Century, Christian churches and leaders have disagreed over such issues as depravity, God's sovereignty, human responsibility, election, predestination, eternal security and the nature and extent of the atonement of Jesus Christ.

Although trained in the reformed tradition, Arminius had serious doubts about the doctrine of "sovereign grace" as taught by the followers of John Calvin. He was a pastor of the Reformed congregation in Amsterdam (1588), but during his fifteen years of ministry there, he began to question many of the conclusions of Calvinism. He left the pastorate and became professor of theology at the University of Leyden. It was his series of lectures on election and predestination that led to a violent and tragic controversy. After his death in 1609, his followers developed the Remonstrance of 1610 which outlined the "Five Points of Arminianism." This document was a protest against the doctrines of the Calvinists, and was submitted to the State of Holland. In 1618, a National Synod of the Church was convened in Dort to examine the teachings of Arminius in the light of Scripture. After 154 sessions, lasting seven months, the Five Points of Arminianism were declared to be heretical. After the synod, many of the disciples of Arminius, such as Hugo Grotius, were imprisoned or banished. When John Wesley took up some of the teachings of Arminianism, the movement began to grow, and it affected the Methodist tradition as well as the beliefs of most Pentecostal and Charismatic churches.

The "Five Points of Arminianism" included the following:

FREE WILL
Arminius believed that the fall of man was not total, maintaining that there was enough good left in man for him to will to accept Jesus Christ unto salvation.

CONDITIONAL ELECTION
Arminius believed that election was based on the foreknowledge of God as to who would believe. Man's "act of

faith" was seen as the "condition" for his being elected to eternal life, since God foresaw him exercising his "free will" in response to Jesus Christ.

UNIVERSAL ATONEMENT

Arminius held that redemption was based on the fact that God loves everybody, that Christ died for everyone, and that the Father is not willing that any should perish. The death of Christ provided the grounds for God to save all men, but each must exercise his own "free will" in order to be saved.

OBSTRUCTABLE GRACE

Arminius believed that since God wanted all men to be saved, He sent the Holy Spirit to "woo" all men to Christ, but since man has absolute "free will," he is able to resist God's will for his life. He believed that God's will to save all men can be frustrated by the finite will of man. He also taught that man exercises his own will first, and then is born again.

FALLING FROM GRACE

If man cannot be saved by God unless it is man's will to be saved, then man cannot continue in salvation unless he continues to will to be saved.

Interestingly, John Calvin, the French reformer, did not formulate what today we know as the Five Points of Calvinism. This came out of the Canons of the Council of Dort (1618), and subsequent statements among the many Reformed Confessions have expanded upon these matters. Calvinism has been known for outstanding scholars, theologians, preachers, and reformers, men such as John Owen, George Whitefield, William Wilberforce, Abraham Kuyper, Charles Hodge, B.B. Warfield, J. Gresham Machen, and Charles Haddon Spurgeon.

Those in the reformed tradition who answered the teachings of Arminius chose the word "TULIP" as an acrostic to summarize their answer to the Five Points of Arminianism:

T = TOTAL DEPRAVITY

The Calvinists believed that man is in absolute bondage to sin and Satan, unable to exercise his own will to trust in Jesus Christ without the help of God.

U = UNCONDITIONAL ELECTION

The Calvinists believed that foreknowledge is based upon the plan and purpose of God, and that election is not based upon the decision of man, but the "free will" of the Creator alone.

L = LIMITED ATONEMENT

The Calvinists believed that Jesus Christ died to save those who were given to Him by the Father in eternity past. In their view, all for whom Jesus died (the elect) will be saved, and all for whom He did not die (the non elect) will be lost.

I = IRRESISTIBLE GRACE

The Calvinists believed that the Lord possesses irresistible grace that cannot be obstructed. They taught that the free will of man is so far removed from salvation, that the elect are regenerated (made spiritually alive) by God even before expressing faith in Jesus Christ for salvation. If a totally depraved person wasn't made alive by the Holy Spirit, such a calling on God would be impossible.

P = PERSEVERANCE OF THE SAINTS

The Calvinists believed that salvation is entirely the work of the Lord, and that man has absolutely nothing to do with the process. The saints will persevere because God will see to it that He will finish the work He has begun.

It is not our purpose to take sides on these issues or to divide the body of Jesus Christ over human interpretations of these

Biblical truths concerning our salvation. We simply desire to state how we in the Calvary Chapel fellowships understand the Bible's teaching regarding these matters.

DEPRAVITY

We believe that all are sinners (Romans 3:23) and unable by human performance to earn, deserve, or merit salvation (Titus 3:5). We believe that the wages of sin is death (Romans 6:23), and that apart from God's grace, no one can be saved (Ephesians 2:8–9). We believe that none are righteous, or capable of doing good (Romans 3:10–12), and that apart from the conviction and regeneration of the Holy Spirit, none can be saved (John 1:12–13; 16:8–11; 1 Peter 1:23–25). Mankind is clearly fallen and lost in sin.

ELECTION

We believe that God chose the believer before the foundation of the world (Ephesians 1:4–6), and based on His foreknowledge, has predestined the believer to be conformed to the image of His Son (Romans 8:29–30). We believe that God offers salvation to all who will call on His name. Romans 10:13 says, "For whosoever shall call on the name of the Lord shall be saved." We also believe that God calls to Himself those who will believe in His Son, Jesus Christ (I Corinthians 1:9). However, the Bible also teaches that an invitation (or call) is given to all, but that only a few will accept it. We see this balance throughout scripture. Revelation 22:17 states, "And whosoever will, let him take the water of life freely." I Peter 1:2 tells us we are, "elect according to the foreknowledge of God, the Father, through sanctification of the Spirit, unto obedience and sprinkling of the blood of Jesus Christ." Matthew 22:14 says, "For many are called, but few are chosen (elected)." God clearly does choose, but man must also accept God's invitation to salvation.

ATONEMENT

We believe that Jesus Christ died as a propitiation (a satisfaction of the righteous wrath of God against sin) "for the whole world" (I John 2:2; 4:9–10), and that He redeems and forgives all who will believe in the death and resurrection of Jesus Christ as their only hope of salvation from sin, death, and hell (Ephesians 1:7; 1 Peter 1:18–19). We believe that eternal life is a gift of God (Romans 6:23), and that "whosoever believeth" in Jesus Christ will not perish, but will have eternal life (John 3:16–18). I Timothy 4:10 says "we trust in the living God, who is the Savior of all men, specially of those that believe." Hebrews 2:9 states that Jesus, "was made a little lower than the angels for the suffering of death, crowned with glory and honor, that He, by the grace of God, should taste death for every man." The atoning sacrifice of Jesus Christ was clearly sufficient to save the entire human race.

GRACE

We believe that God's grace is not the result of human effort or worthiness (Romans 3:24–28; 11:6), but is the response of God's mercy and love to those who will believe in His Son (Ephesians 2:4–10). Grace gives to us what we do not deserve nor can earn by our performance (Romans 11:6). We believe that God's grace and mercy can be resisted by us. Jesus said in Matthew 23:37, "O Jerusalem, Jerusalem, thou that killest the prophets, and stonest them who are sent unto thee, how often would I have gathered thy children together, even as a hen gathereth her chickens under her wings, and ye would not." We are not condemned because we have no opportunity to be saved, but a person is condemned because he makes a choice not to believe (John 3:18). In John 5:40 we read "And ye will not come to Me, that ye might have life." Jesus also said in John 6:37, "All that the Father giveth Me shall come to Me; and him that cometh to Me I will in no wise cast out." John 6:40 states, "And this is the will of Him that sent Me, that everyone who seeth the Son, and believeth on Him, may have everlasting life." In John 7:37 Jesus said, "If any man thirst, let him come unto Me, and drink." In John 11:26 He adds, "whosoever liveth and believeth in Me shall never die."

Jesus clearly acknowledges the fact of human resistance and rejection. In John 12:46–48 He said,

"I am come as a light into the world, that whosoever believeth on Me should not abide in darkness. And if any man hear My words, and believe not, I judge him not; for I came, not to judge the world but to save the world. He that rejecteth Me, and receiveth not My words, hath One that judgeth him: the word that I have spoken, the same shall judge him in the last day."

In Stephen's message in Acts 7:51, he concluded by saying, "Ye stiff–necked and uncircumcised in heart and ears, ye do always resist the Holy Ghost; as your fathers did, so do ye." In Romans 10:21, the apostle Paul quotes Isaiah 65:2 when he speaks of God's words to Israel, "All day long I have stretched forth My hands unto a disobedient and gainsaying people." In one of the five warning passages of the book of Hebrews, we read in Hebrews 10:26,

"For if we sin willfully after we have received the knowledge of the truth, there remaineth no more sacrifice for sins." Verse 29 adds, "Of how much sorer punishment, suppose ye, shall he be thought worthy, who hath trodden under foot the Son of God, and hath counted the blood of the covenant, with which he was sanctified, an unholy thing, and hath done despite unto the Spirit of grace?"

Clearly, God's grace can either be resisted or received by the exercise of human free will.

PERSEVERANCE

We believe that nothing can separate us from the love of God in Jesus Christ our Lord (Romans 8:38–39), and that there is no condemnation to those who are in Jesus Christ (Romans 8:1). We believe that the promise of Jesus in John 10:27–28 is clear: "My sheep hear My voice, and I know them, and they follow Me. And I give unto them eternal life; and they shall never perish, neither shall any man pluck them out of My hand." Jesus said in John 6:37, "him that cometh to Me I will in no wise cast out." We have this assurance in Philippians 1:6, "Being confident of this very thing, that He who hath begun a good work in you will perform it until the day of Jesus Christ." We believe that the Holy Spirit has sealed us unto the day of redemption (Ephesians 1:13–14; 4:30).

But we also are deeply concerned over the words of Jesus in Matthew 7:21–23:

"Not every one that saith unto Me, Lord, Lord, shall enter into the kingdom of heaven, but he that doeth the will of my Father, who is in heaven. Many will say to Me in that day, Lord, Lord, have we not prophesied in Thy name? And in Thy name have cast out devils? And in Thy name done many wonderful works? And then will I profess unto them, I never knew you; depart from Me, ye that work iniquity."

Apparently there are many who claim to be believers that in fact are not.

Jesus said in Luke 9:62, "No man, having put his hand to the plough, and looking back, is fit for the kingdom of God." I Corinthians 6:9–10 insists that "the unrighteous shall not inherit the kingdom of God" and warns us not to be deceived. A list is then given of various kinds of sinful lifestyles with an ending remark that they will not inherit the kingdom of God. Similar statements and conclusions are given in Galatians 5:19–21 and Ephesians 5:3–5.

Galatians 5:4 says "Christ is become of no effect unto you, whosoever of you are justified by the law; ye are fallen from grace." Colossians 1:22–23 says about Jesus Christ "In the body of his flesh through death, to present you holy and unblameable and unreproveable in His sight, if ye continue in the faith grounded and settled, and be not moved away from the hope of the gospel, which ye have heard, and which was preached to every creature that is under heaven, of which I, Paul, am made a minister." II Timothy 2:12 says "if we deny Him, He also will deny us." Hebrews 3:12 says, "Take heed, brethren, lest there be in any of you an evil heart of unbelief, in departing from the living God." Can true believers ("brethren") depart from the living God? I Timothy 4:1 says that "in the latter times, some shall depart from the faith." II Thessalonians 2:3 speaks of "a falling away" or an apostasy. II Peter 2:20–21 makes these remarkable statements:

"For if, after they have escaped the pollutions of the world through the knowledge of the Lord and Savior, Jesus Christ, they are again entangled in it, and overcome, the latter end is worse with them than the beginning. For it had been better for them not to have known the way of righteousness than, after they have known it, to turn from the holy commandment delivered unto them."

It is no wonder that Peter says in II Peter 1:10, "Wherefore the rather, brethren, give diligence to make your calling and election sure; for if ye do these things, ye shall never fall." We thank God for the encouragement of Jude 24, "Now unto Him that is able to keep you from falling, and to present you faultless before the presence of His glory with exceeding joy."

Maintaining a Bible-centered balance in these difficult issues is of great importance. We do believe in the perseverance of the saints (true believers), but are deeply concerned about sinful lifestyles and rebellious hearts among those who call themselves "Christians." We don't have all the answers to these matters, but we desire to be faithful to the Lord and His word. If we find ourselves basing our view of salvation on the performance and attitudes of people we become discouraged and concerned. But when we keep our eyes on the Lord, and trust in Him alone and in His power, we say with Peter in I Peter 1:3–9:

> "Blessed be the God and Father of our Lord Jesus Christ, who, according to His abundant mercy, hath begotten us again unto a lively hope by the resurrection of Jesus Christ from the dead, to an inheritance incorruptible, and undefiled, and that fadeth not away, reserved in heaven for you, who are kept by the power of God through faith unto salvation ready to be revealed in the last time. In this ye greatly rejoice, though now for a season, if need be, ye are in heaviness through manifold temptations, that the trial of your faith, being much more precious than of gold that perisheth, though it be tried with fire, might be found unto praise and honor and glory at the appearing of Jesus Christ, whom, having not seen, ye love; in whom, though now ye see Him not, yet believing, ye rejoice with joy unspeakable and full of glory, receiving the end of your faith, even the salvation of your souls."

It is not easy to maintain the unity of the Spirit among us on these matters. It seems that the sovereignty of God and human responsibility are like two parallel lines that do not seem to intersect within our finite minds. God's ways are "past finding out" (Romans 11:33), and the Bible warns us to "lean not unto thy own understanding" (Proverbs 3:5). To say what God says in the Bible – no more and no less – is not always easy, comfortable, or completely understandable. But Scripture tells us that the wisdom from above will be loving and kind toward all, seeking the unity of the believers, not trying to find ways to divide and separate from one another. May God help us all to love each other, to be kind, tenderhearted, forgiving one another as Jesus Christ has forgiven us (Ephesians 4:32)! In difficult doctrinal matters, may we have gracious attitudes and humble hearts, desiring most of all to please Him who has called us to serve Him in the body of Christ. Discussion – YES! Disagreements – YES! Division – NO!

Jesus said, "By their fruit ye shall know them." When a particular position on the Scriptures causes one to become argumentative, legalistic, and divisive, I question the validity of that position. I seek to embrace those things that tend to make me more loving and kind, more forgiving and merciful. I know then that I am becoming more like my Lord. If you have come to a strong personal conviction on one side of a doctrinal issue, please grant us the privilege of first seeing how it has helped you to become more Christ–like in your nature, and then we will judge whether we need to come to that same persuasion. Let us always be certain to look at the fruit of the teaching.

Seek those things that produce the loving nature of Jesus in our lives. I would rather have the wrong facts and a right attitude, than right facts and a wrong attitude. God can change my understanding of the facts in a moment, but it often takes a lifetime to effect changes of attitude.

Yours in love,

Chuck Smith

OTHER TITLES BY CHUCK SMITH

THE MAN GOD USES
Item #: BKTMG01PB

Do you want to be used by God? In this inspiring new book, Pastor Chuck examines the personal characteristics of the apostles as they were used in the first chapters of The Book of Acts. What set these people apart to be used by God? With remarkable insight, Chuck reveals that answer and more. 144 pages.

LIVING WATER
Item #: BKLWA01PB

This book captures the message of God's ability to change lives through His Holy Spirit. The reader will grow deeply in their knowledge and understanding of the Holy Spirit; His grace, His love, His power, and His gifts. 297 pages.

WHY GRACE CHANGES EVERYTHING
Item #: BKWGC01

Through remarkable insight gleaned from his own life, Pastor Chuck unfolds the mystery of grace and reveals many surprising truths. The reader will be refreshed and encouraged by the depth of God's grace toward us. 218 pages.

CALVARY CHAPEL DISTINCTIVES
Item #: BKCCD01

In Calvary Chapel we value both the teaching of God's Word, as well as the work of the Holy Spirit. This book explains the balance that makes Calvary Chapel a distinct and uniquely blessed movement of God. 142 pages.

HARVEST
Item #: BKHAR01PB

Telling the growth of Calvary Chapel, this book features the life and testimonies of Chuck Smith and nine other Calvary Chapel pastors. God called these leaders, just as He has called you. Read this inspiring story of evangelism, discipleship and faith. 147 pages.

CHARISMA VS. CHARISMANIA
Item #: BKCVC01

Chuck Smith gives a scripturally balanced look at the person and work of the Holy Spirit. He carefully points out the difference between true charisma and the "Charismatic experience." 142 pages.

EFFECTIVE PRAYER LIFE
Item #: BKCBA10

Practical studies in prayer that equip and help you to have a more effective and dynamic prayer life. An excellent resource for personal growth and group discipleship. 102 pages.

THE GOSPEL ACCORDING TO GRACE
Item #: BKTGA01

A clear and enlightening commentary on the Book of Romans. Chuck Smith reviews Paul's epistle, one of the most important books in the Bible, on a verse-by-verse basis. 231 pages.

ANSWERS FOR TODAY
Item #: BKAFT01

This is a compilation of the popular Answer Pamphlet series in paperback form. It includes "It's Time for the Sunrise," "Questions & Answers," "Unto Us a Son Is Given," "A More Sure Word," "The Rapture," and many others. 247 pages.

THE FINAL CURTAIN
Item #: BKCBA12

This recently updated book deals with such subjects as Bible prophecy, the Middle East, Russia, and the role of the Antichrist. Also included is a helpful glossary with terms relating to the Bible and prophecy. 132 pages.

THE CLAIMS OF CHRIST
Item #: PATCO01

Chuck Smith gives a straightforward presentation of the claims of Jesus Christ, along with proof of their validity. Readers are challenged to accept or reject the claims of Christ. 24 pages.

WHAT THE WORLD IS COMING TO
Item #: BKWTW01

What is the world coming to? The answer is documented in the Book of Revelation: a prophetic and unerring account of man's final days on earth. This book is a complete commentary on the book of Revelation and the scenario for the last days. 215 pages.

THE TRIBULATION AND THE CHURCH
Item #: BKTTA01

Will the church of Christ experience the Great Tribulation? This book expounds upon biblical prophecy and future events while looking at the church. 71 pages.

COMFORT, FOR THOSE WHO MOURN
Item #: PACFT01

In this pamphlet, Pastor Chuck shares the glorious hope we have in the resurrection of Jesus Christ and how we can find comfort through Him during a time of loss. 28 pages.

REDEMPTION
Item #: PARED01

In this clear and easy to read commentary, Pastor Chuck explores and explains the concept of our redemption in Christ using the story of Ruth and her "Goel"or savior, Boaz. 24 pages.

CALVINISM, ARMINIANISM & THE WORD OF GOD
Item #: PACAA01

This pamphlet discusses the facts upon which these two doctrinal stands are based, and compares them to the Word of God. 20 pages.

For ordering information, please contact:

THE WORD FOR TODAY

P.O. BOX 8000, COSTA MESA, CA 92628

(800) 272-WORD (9673)

WWW.TWFT.COM

NOTES